Ziz's Cookbook

An Italian American Dad's Guide
to Cooking with Love & Tradition:

Mangia! Buon Appetito! Enjoy!

by Chris Zizza

DORRANCE
PUBLISHING CO
EST. 1920
PITTSBURGH, PENNSYLVANIA 15238

Dorrance Publishing Co
585 Alpha Drive
Suite 103
Pittsburgh, PA 15238
Visit our website at *www.dorrancebookstore.com*

ISBN: 978-1-6386-7017-9
eISBN: 978-1-6386-7966-0

Ziz's Cookbook

An Italian American Dad's Guide
to Cooking with Love & Tradition:

Mangia! Buon Appetito! Enjoy!

This book is dedicated to my mother, Judi Zizza and my Grand-mother, Jeanette Giambanco.

Thank you for the tradition of cooking in our family, and thank you for passing on your recipes to the generations that follow. Chris Zizza

Judi Zizza

Jeanette Giambanco

We all did our best over the years to get as much information as possible from my mother, my aunt, and my grandmother. When asking about the measurements or the ingredients, here are some of the answers we would get ...

Question: How many eggs?
Answer: "Two ... but you might need three."
Question: How much salt?
Answer: "Just a little, unless you need more."
Question: How much parsley?
Answer: "The same amount as last time."
Question: How much grated cheese?
Answer: "Not so much that it tastes cheesy."
Question: How thin do I roll the dough?
Answer: "Thin enough."

Table of Contents

MAMA Z's Ricotta Gnocchi

INGREDIENTS
1 15oz container of Ricotta
3 egg yolks
1 cup of all purpose flour
3/4 cup of freshly grated Romano or Parmesan
Salt to taste

Take paper towels and empty Ricotta on top. Take more paper towels and cover ricotta entirely.

Without too much pressure pat the ricotta dry. You may need to change the paper towels several times to be sure it is as dry as possible.

In a large mixing bowl add the Ricotta and all the remaining ingredients using a spoon at first. After the ingredients are well mixed use your hands to be sure all ingredients are blended together.

Take a small amount of the mix and roll on a board that is coated lightly with flour. Roll into a long tube and make the tube about the thickness of a pencil.

Using a butter knife cut into small pieces and place on wax paper.

When all your gnocchi is cut boil water with salt and add to the boiling water. About 3 minutes and they will be done.

Serve with sauce or pesto and Enjoy!

These will also freeze very well so double the recipe and save some in the freezer for another Day

The Best Steak EVER!
Flip the Script with the Reverse Sear!

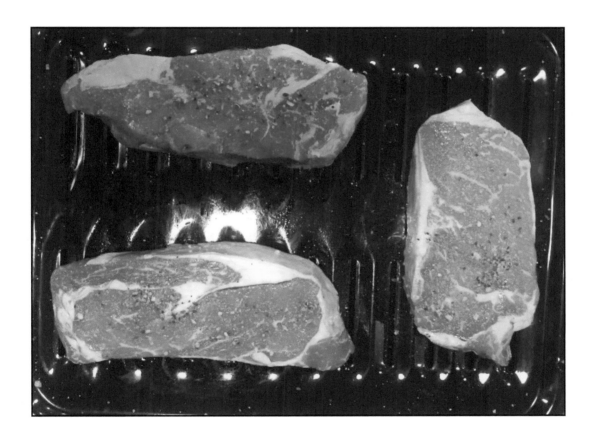

Start in the Oven and Finish with A Sear

Start with a Salt-and-Pepper Crust: put plenty of salt all around the steak on every side, then add pepper as well, just enough pepper to your liking, but you can never put too much salt to seal the juices.

Put on oven rack at a preheat of 275° F.

Pull from oven at interior temp 125° F.

Note: An interior temp of 125° F is medium rare,

Maybe 25–30 minutes, or use a probe meter

After reaching 125° F, remove from the oven and let it rest for 15 min.

After resting, put into a HOT cast-iron skillet and sear for 1–2 minutes each side

And serve HOT!

Cook veggies in a separate baking sheet at the same time. While the steak cooks, do your veggies for 30–45 minutes at 275° F, produces some tasty veggies!

Veggie Notes and Suggestions

I use an olive oil spray on my veggies.

After prepping veggies, put them in the baking pan and salt them and spray them with oil and season to your liking.

Check on them while they cook and add seasoning as desired.

Note: The veggies need to be mixed up while cooking or they dry out.

Continue cooking the veggies while the steak is resting.

Bird in a Basket

A favorite of mine growing up, and after becoming a dad, I was only too happy to pass this favorite along to my own children.

First, start with a good size slice of bread.

Next, you will need something to cut a circle right in the middle of the slice of bread.

It needs to be about 2 1/2″ in diameter.

They make different-shaped cookie cutters, but I just use a circle shape from the kitchen. (Hint: you can use the top of a glass if you don't have a round cookie cutter.)

Cut a hole in the center of the bread and put the circle of bread aside for now.

Heat up a fry pan and drop in some butter.

Take the bread and drop it into the butter, moving it around so you get the bread buttered well and flip it so it's buttered on both sides (add more butter if necessary).

Now crack an egg in the middle of the circle and let it start to cook.

While the egg is cooking, butter both sides of your cut-out circle of bread and place bread slice all at once and let it cook, much like an over-easy egg.

Note: You need to watch out that the bread does not burn.

Flip the circle when ready as well.

When done, place the slice on the plate and the circle on top of the egg and SERVE. :)

Note: I use a serrated knife and cut in strips to open the yolk and then put the circle back on top.

You can serve it whole or sliced; the choice is yours (but my kids like it cut up with the circle on top).

Note: if you prefer the egg scrambled, that's fine, just scramble the egg first and cook the same way

My daughter Emma always liked scrambled,
and Ava always liked the over-easy…Enjoy!

Time to Make Some Manicotti
444 Cooking party with Auntie Cay and Uncle Georgie in August 2016

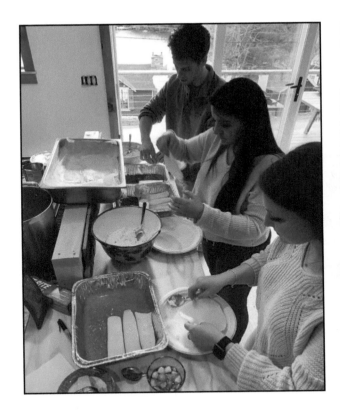

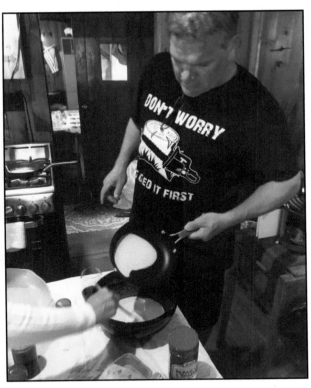

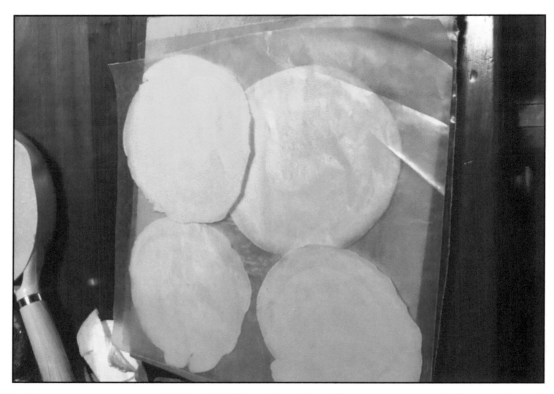

Using a proper 7″ skillet is the key to making fresh, homemade Manicotti.

Ziz's Mom's Manicotti Recipe

Shell Batter (Crepe) - 1 Batch = 18–20 total crepes

Ingredients:
Small fry pan, about 7" rim
1 cup Flour (all-purpose King Arthur)
1 cup Water (1 cup strong = 10oz.)
3 Eggs

Mix eggs, flour, and water with a whisk and leave no lumps—add extra flour or water to ensure a loose, watery consistency.

With a medium-sized gravy spoon or small ladle (about 2 Tbsp.), ladle 1 scoop into pan (note: make sure you spray pan with Pam).

Cook until crepe is cooked enough that it is not watery and dry around the edges (not burned but dry); the edges will curve up slightly when done. Slide out of pan onto wax paper and let cool off just a little

Filling: 2 lbs. Ricotta and some Parsley with 2–3 Eggs and some grated Romano Cheese

Mix with a spoon until smooth (no need to beat eggs, just crack, drop, and mix until they all blend in).

Place about a tablespoon into the center of crepe and fold over until covered, then fold over again and place with seam facing down on the cookie sheet or pan.

Filling should be only in the center while the ends should be empty about 3/4"–1" on each end.

Note 1: Only one layer when placing on pan, no stacking on top of each other when storing for the freezer. Freeze until ready to cook…

Note 2: Do not make crepes and sit in the fridge—you must make and freeze manicotti for later or make and cook all on the same day…

Letting them sit without any preservatives unfrozen for a long period of time is not a good idea.

Note 3: All ingredients above made 3 batches of Manicotti (60 total pieces).

Baking
(Don't let them defrost; it makes them sticky and gummy.)

Put a layer of sauce on the bottom of a pan and one layer of Frozen Manicotti.

Next, cover Frozen Manicotti with sauce and a little grated Cheese.

Cover with foil, punch some holes in the foil... Bake at 350° F for 30 minutes; let sit for a few minutes.

"Mange, Bon Appetite"

Pastina

Whenever I was sick, my brother, my sister, or any of my cousins...Pastina fixed it every time...

Ingredients:
3 quarts of Water (if thick is desired) or
3 1/2 quarts of Water (if you want it more like a broth)
7 (small) Chicken Bouillon Cubes
Salt and Basil (season to your liking)
A little Oil (always a little oil)
1 Egg

Boil the water and bouillon cubes, stirring every few minutes, and then dump in the pastina when it starts to boil, and just when it's done, about 6 minutes later, scramble an egg and slowly drizzle it through a fork so it drips into the mix all over the top and let it cook in... Serve a few minutes later...

Blow on it... It's hot!

Ziz's Mom's Sauce

Ingredients:
Fillipo Berrio Extra Virgin Olive Oil
Tuttorosso Crushed Tomatoes (ONLY Tuttorosso) (2–4 cans, depends on the batch size you want)
Tomato Paste, 1 can (any brand with the paste)
Fresh Garlic, 2–3 cloves
Fresh Onion, 1 small or a 1/2 large, sweet onion
Basil and Parsley, season to your liking
Salt and Pepper, season to your liking
Water (1 can added using the tomato paste can)
Pork, use 1 or 2 small boneless pork chops
Meatballs (see Meatball recipe in this book)
Sausage (I like Sweet Italian, but you do you)

The Sauce Process
Add oil to saucepan, enough to just cover the bottom of pan and heat.

Chop onions (small) and slice garlic (extremely thin).

Add onions and garlic to oil (pay attention, as you cannot burn this or start over).

Add basil and parsley, salt, pepper and cook about 5 minutes with the simmering garlic and onions.

Add tomato paste and 1 can of water using can from tomato paste.

Stir, and after a minute, add crushed tomatoes (all cans); rinse with a touch of water and pour into the sauce so you get it all in there. No need to waste any.

Add more basil and parsley, salt, and pepper as desired.

Allow to cook a little on medium. Next, brown the pork, sausage, and meatballs in a frying pan with a little oil.

(Always a little oil; you're cooking Italian now.)

Don't cook the meat too much! Just want to brown them lightly.

(Brown the sausage a little more than the meat.)

Add the meat to the sauce after browning, and now bring the heat to low and allow to cook all day or at least 2–4 hours. Check on it and stir periodically.

Put in the fridge overnight, and the next morning, heat up on the stove until hot and then lower to simmer.

This is only if you made the sauce the day before (it really gains flavor when you let it sit overnight).

While on simmer, allow it to cook for a couple hours.

Let sit on stove until ready to eat, stir occasionally, but don't damage the meatballs.

Occasionally test the sauce by dipping bread when you walk by; it's a right of passage when you're Italian!

Braciolettini is the best for any backyard BBQ or Tailgate Party, Trust ME!

Braciolettini

Ingredients:
Eye of the Round Roast
Fillipo Berrio Oil
Marinated Mushrooms
Marinated Roasted Red Peppers
Progresso Italian-Style Breadcrumbs
Parmesan and Romano Grated Cheese
Parsley
Toothpicks

Braciolettini

What to do: (prep) First, trim all fat off the eye of the round; then using a slicer, cut meat into very thin slices (maybe 1/8").

Dice the mushrooms and the peppers.

Mix 4 cups of breadcrumbs with 2 cups of the grated cheese and 2 oz. of parsley.

Now in a smaller bowl, mix some of the newly mixed breadcrumbs and cheese "stuffing" with some oil.

Add the oil to the level of what would look like a "wet sand."

Next...pour a small amount of oil in a saucer dish and dip the slice of meat slightly and lay flat on a cutting board (flatten it out, rubbing the oil onto both sides).

Now with the meat laid out flat, put roughly a heaping tablespoon in the middle and smooth it around and add some diced peppers and mushrooms.

To roll it: take it from the bottom, grab the meat at one end, and roll it away from you and hold it together with a toothpick...

When complete, put finished product into a tray until it's time to cook.

Then place the rolled meat into a grilling basket and cook to your liking.

(Note: they cook fast ... maybe 2 minutes on each side.)

Enjoy!

Dampen with oil and spread it out thin.

Add the stuffing spread it out flat and roll.

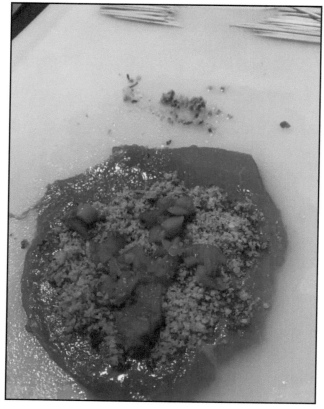

After rolling it, use a toothpick to hold it together.

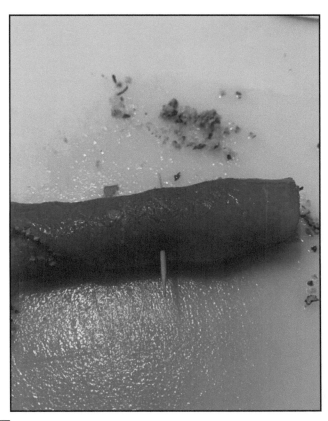

You can use your own slicer, or in some stores, the butcher will slice it for you, but don't forget to ask him to trim the fat off, and don't let him cut it too thick.

Braciolettini

Ziz's Grandmother's Meatballs Jeanette Giambanco (aka papa)

Ingredients for 16—18 meatballs
(2 lbs. meat)
Italian Bread, 2 slices per Lb. (add more if desired)
Italian Breadcrumbs if needed (1—2 Tbsp.)
Parsley ("enough" LOL) maybe 2 Tbsp.
Onion salt 1/2 Tbsp.
Garlic salt 1 tsp.
Eggs (1 egg/lb.)
80/20 Ground Burger Meat (2 lb.)
Water, as needed
Grated Cheese, 3 Tbsp.

Take the crust off the bread and soak in water to make bread moist.

2 slices of bread for each lb. of meat.

Next, add the meat and mix by hand (2 lbs.).

Add the onion salt, the garlic salt, and 2 eggs and mix by hand.

Add grated cheese, 3 Tbsp., and mix by hand.

Add parsley and mix by hand.

NOTE: add water if too dry.

You want the mix to be smooth and consistent, not dry and bulky or bumpy—it should stick together like a soft paste (but not too wet).

Next, spray a broiler pan and make round meatballs by hand and place on broil pan for 4 minutes and turn them and check in 4 more minutes, and when ready, drop them in the sauce for 1–2 hours and serve!

Fresh Pasta for Ravioli

(you can use a processor to mix)

Ingredients:
Eggs
Regular Flour and Semolina Flour
Oil
Salt
Water
Just mix ingredients until smooth and then run through pasta machine
1 lb. flour/5 eggs
A little oil and a little water and salt
Semolina flour for dusting so you're not too sticky

Ravioli Time! It must be Thanksgiving!

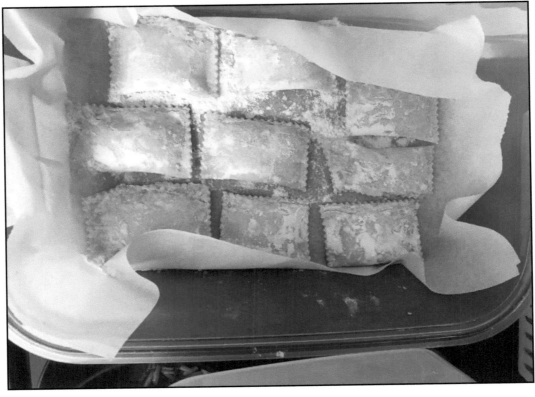

My Mother's Ravioli is a Thanksgiving Day Tradition. She would make them every year with her sister, my Aunt Marie Fabiano (aka Ree-ree).

When we were kids, my brother, my sister, and I would help, and we would sit at the table and eat the pasta dough scraps as it was being trimmed away.

I am proud to see the tradition continue here with our next generation of family chefs, made up of my two daughters, Emma and Ava, all my nieces and nephews and my cousins.

The pictures in these pages really show how a love for cooking can bring a family together!

Ziz's Mom's Ravioli

Part 1: The Dough (We use a food processor to mix.)
3 Eggs
3 cups Flour
1 tsp Oil
a pinch of Salt
a touch of Water

Mix it all into dough.
When done, wrap in plastic wrap and let it sit for 15–30 minutes.

Part 2: The Filling
Make filling using freshly chopped parsley (chopped small, really small), about 1–2 oz. or your preference.

32 oz. ricotta cheese, 2 eggs to start; if dry, add a third egg.

Some grated Romano cheese just some over the top, a pinch or 2 of salt, and mix all together.

Cut 1/3 off of the dough and run it through the pasta maker to get it flat.

Not so flat that you get holes and not so thick that you can't fold it…

Then lay it on the counter on top of some flour and stretch it out.

Now put dollops of filling all the way down the strip and then fold it over and press together the edges.

Then, using your finger, push down between dollops to make individual ravioli pieces and trim with crimped pastry wheel.

Repeat until out of dough and place on a floured parchment paper and place in the freezer.

Once they are frozen, you can switch into a freezer-ready Ziplock bag.

Each batch makes about 30 ravioli, or in my mother's words,

"Each batch makes enough for some people; if you run short, make more."

Mahi Mahi

Fun and easy, and hopefully you caught it yourself!

Ingredients:
Fresh Mahi Mahi (also known as Dolphin, the fish)
Salt and Pepper
Butter and Parsley (yup, that's it)

Melt a stick of butter and some parsley and salt and pepper in a saucepan, and using a small chip brush, paint the dolphin filet and coat both sides.

Place it on a grill, and as it cooks, continue to butter it.

Maybe 1–2 minutes each side, as it cooks quick, but that also depends on the thickness.

HINT: it is cooked when it turns white and easily breaks apart with a fork.

The Feast of the Seven Fishes is part of the Italian-American Christmas Eve celebration, although it is not called that in Italy and is not a "feast" in the sense of "holiday" but rather a grand meal. Christmas Eve is a vigil or fasting day, and the abundance of seafood reflects the observance of abstinence from meat until the feast of Christmas Day itself.

Today, the meal typically consists of seven different seafood dishes. The tradition comes from southern Italy, where it is known simply as The Vigil (*La Vigilia*). This celebration commemorates the wait, the *Vigilia di Natale*, for the midnight birth of the baby Jesus. It was introduced in the United States by southern Italian immigrants in New York City's Little Italy in the late 1800s.

The long tradition of eating seafood on Christmas Eve dates from the Roman Catholic tradition of abstaining from eating meat on the eve of a feast day. As no meat or animal fat could be used on such days, observant Catholics would instead eat fish (typically fried in oil).

The Feast of the Seven Fishes
A Christmas Eve Family Tradition!

Many ask why seven fishes? Some say it's because of the seven Sacraments or the seven virtues.

Others believe it's because on the seventh day God rested.

To me it matters not. I just love The Feast of the Seven Fishes!

Buon Natale

Merry Christmas

Any fish is fine!

We usually had Lobster, Clams Casino, Smelts, Shrimp, Pasta with Lobster Sauce, Baccala, Cod Fish, King Crab.

The Lounge at 444
Where so many meals have been happily served